Our thanks go to the following people for providing photographs,
illustrations, encouragement and advice:

Peter Double,
Chris Newton Director of Environment,
Michael Dryden and Nick Parlett.

Designed by the Studio
Published by MSP Channel Islands,
a division of the Jersey Evening Post,
PO Box 582, Jersey JE4 8XQ.

First printed November 2004
Second print June 2006
Printed and bound in the United Kingdom

ISBN 0-9539116-5-9

Contents

Introduction

From a migrating reed warbler's point of view, being confronted by seemingly endless miles of open water, after having just completed the flight from northern Africa to the Brittany coast must be a daunting challenge. A built-in navigation system tells the bird the course it should take and, with less than an ounce of body weight providing power, it takes off and heads out to sea.

This astonishing driving force brings many thousands of summer and winter migrants to the Channel Islands and the phenomenon occurs with delightful predictability every year.

Even the most casual naturalist is aware that the arrival or departure of birds provides the islands with a natural and, occasionally, uncannily accurate, clock. The arrival of wheatears, the departure of swifts, the sound of the first cuckoo or the mutterings of Brent geese on the tide line; these are all seasonal indicators, natural milestones in the Channel Islands avian calendar.

Not all our birds are migrants of course. Among the islands is a rich seam of resident species ranging through the whole stratum of habitats. In some cases, those we consider residents are joined in winter by their northern cousins – oystercatchers, coots and even robins will boost resident numbers.

Of those summer migrants that touch the Channel Islands, not all will remain. Thousands of birds merely pass through the islands, using them as a 'convenience store' during their journey north. An early swallow feeding on flies along a Guernsey beach may eventually raise a brood in a barn in the Yorkshire Dales; it is likely that a wheatear taking flies on Alderney's rabbit-cropped turf in March might later raise young in Greenland. The islands do not support a million puffins or experience estuary waders in tens of thousands but, in sheer diversity of species, they are as rich as anywhere in Great Britain and Europe.

The fortunes of birds

In general, the fortunes of birds in the islands reflect those experienced in the rest of Britain. House sparrow, herring gull and song thrush numbers are in decline but, since placing stringent controls on the use of pesticides, peregrine falcon and sparrowhawk numbers have increased. Over the past decade we, like the rest of southern Britain, have enjoyed the gradual northward movement of the little egret. This pure white heron-like bird with its black bill and bright yellow feet has now become a fairly common sight among the reefs and gullies of low tide. In Jersey, no fewer than eleven pairs of egrets raised young during the summer of 2003.
Mild winters can create certain differences between the islands and the rest of Britain. Chiffchaffs will happily over-winter here among heavily wooded valleys and it is not unusual to see sandwich terns in early February, loping over the waters of sheltered bays. Cetti's and Dartford warblers both seem to manage the Channel Islands winters quite well too unless extreme weather and low temperatures occur for lengthy periods.

Arrivals and departures

An influx of tourists increases the population of the Channel Islands enormously during the summer months and many visitors head instinctively for the coast to enjoy a pollution-free environment. In winter, this same clean coastal habitat provides waders and wildfowl with a rich source of energy in the form of worms, crustaceans, molluscs and fish at a time when their northern breeding grounds are ice-bound. The tide line echoes with the sound of curlew, redshank and grey plover and above the gentle surf of sheltered bays and rocky gullies, a mixture of dunlin, sanderling and turnstones perform those wonderful synchronised flights synonymous with the tide line in winter.

With the onset of spring, wintering wader numbers gradually decrease as birds leave for their northern breeding grounds and the summer migrants begin to appear. Generally, the first arrivals will be wheatears on their way from tropical Africa, through Britain and north as far as Iceland and Greenland. Many thousands of birds will use the islands as staging posts, staying just a few days to stock up on the energy that will sustain their onward flight.

As spring progresses the more noticeable summer migrants, sand martins and swallows in particular, begin passing through the islands, followed much later by cuckoo, swift and spotted flycatcher.

The arrival of some birds is less noticeable. Whitethroats, reed and sedge warblers will invariably announce their presence from the cover of thick scrub and reed beds and it is this, combined with the songs of resident species, that gives such a richness and diversity to early summer among the wilder areas of the islands.

Islanders are lucky in that they can enjoy a constantly changing diversity of bird life during all seasons of the year. For some autumn and spring might be highlights but, in a group of islands where thousands of birds are ringed annually and a count of 200 individual bird species is not unusual in a given year, it can be said with confidence that any time is a good time to watch birds in the Channel Islands.

Vagrants, birds that should not, under normal circumstances, be anywhere near the Channel Islands do have a habit of turning up occasionally. A Mediterranean or ring-billed gull among a flock of black-headed gulls, or a honey buzzard drifting over from France on warm thermals. So, one should be prepared to meet rarities on occasion.

Exotics and escapes are not unknown in the Channel Islands. A pink smudge on a

far tide line may well be a Chilean flamingo. Birds such as whooper swans, red-breasted and barnacle geese ticked at local wetland sites could have been bred in captivity among the islands and may simply have decided on a change of scenery. Most local 'birders' enjoy these occasional appearances but generally they are regarded with a certain reserve unless their wild status can be proved without doubt.

Bird habitats

The bird habitats of the Channel Islands can be separated into six major categories:

Maritime heath and dry grassland
Cliffs and offshore islets
The tide line
Woodlands
Freshwater wetlands
Farmland, parks and gardens

On small islands such as ours there is a continuous overlap of birds into habitats where they might not normally be expected. Carrion crows are regularly seen on beaches at low tide lifting and dropping cockles; in winter, starlings, meadow pipits, black redstarts and even robins will happily join turnstones, pied wagtails and rock pipits catching flies among piles of sun-warmed vraic on the high tide line. Blackbirds and wrens, too, seem just as content on cliffs and heathland as in parks and gardens.

There are, however, bird species that will conform to those habitats in which one would expect to find them. Dartford warblers only frequent heathland gorse thickets, ravens and peregrine falcons will best be found along rugged coastal cliffs and house sparrows will always prefer an environment close to, or even in, human habitation.

One might sum up this overlapping tendency of birds and habitats by suggesting that, when walking anywhere in the islands, always expect the unexpected because you are just as likely to see a kingfisher hunting for whitebait in a rocky coastal bay as among reed-fringed ponds inland.

So, what birds can we expect to see among the diverse habitats of the Channel Islands.

Where to look – Alderney

Maritime heath and dry grassland
Giffoine
Essex Hill
Val du Saou
Longis Common

Cliffs and offshore islets
From a boat, Burhou, Ortac, les Etac
Coque
Lihou
All cliff areas south of Alderney

The tide line
Braye bay
Longis bay
Clonque bay

Woodlands
Bonne Terre
Vaux du Fret
Val du Saou

Freshwater wetlands
Longis pond is the obvious one with water rail etc, but also worth considering is Mannez Pond where we are trying to establish a reed bed for breeding birds

Farmland, parks and gardens
Blaye (bramble covered banks)
Western Blaye
Valley Gardens and Terrace

Where to look – Guernsey

Maritime heath and dry grassland
Pleinmont
L'Ancresse Common
Fort Le Merchant

Cliff and offshore islets
From Fermain Bay in the east to Pleinmont in the west

The tide line
From Rocquaine Bay in the south west to Belle Greve Bay in the east

Woodlands
Talbot Valley
Fauxquet Valley
Petit Bot
Saints Valley

Freshwater wetlands
Vale Pond
La Claire Mare
St Saviours Reservoir

Farmland, parks and gardens
Sausmarez Park
Farmland is a major feature of the upper parishes of St Saviour,
St Pierre du Bois and Torteval

Where to look - Herm

Maritime heath and dry grassland
The Common

Cliff and offshore islets
South and south east cliffs

The tide line
From the harbour around the north of the island to Belvoir Bay

Farmland, parks and gardens
The central ridge of the island is farmland

Where to look - Jersey

Maritime heath and dry grassland
Noirmont Headland
Portelet Headland
L'Ouaisne Common
The south west coast from Les Creux to La Corbiere
The whole of the west coast - La Pulente to L'Etacq
Les Landes from L'Etacq to Gréve de Lecq

Cliffs and offshore islets
South west coast - Noirmont Headland to La Corbiere
The north west and north coasts - Les Landes to La Rozel harbour

The tide line
Gorey to St Helier harbour
St Aubin's Bay
Petit Port bay
L'Etacq

Woodlands
Rozel Woods
St Peter's Valley
Waterworks Valley
NB: Many of Jersey's sheltered valleys provide woodland habitat and offer the opportunity to see a variety of bird species

Freshwater wetlands
Rozel Woods
Grouville Marsh
Queen's Valley Reservoir
St Peter's Valley ponds and reservoirs
Waterworks Valley reservoirs
St Ouen's Pond

Farmland, parks and gardens
Jersey's country parishes are rich in farmland and hedge-lined country lanes and provide plenty of bird watching opportunities. The park-like footpaths surrounding two of the Island's major reservoirs - Queen's Valley and Val de la Mare - are also recommended

Where to look - Sark

Surrounded by cliffs plus farmland and fields

Habitat 1
Maritime heath and dry grassland

In many areas of the Channel Islands heather, gorse, lichens and a myriad of insects dominate the land adjacent to steep cliffs. Often, coastal paths cut through a habitat where the landscape has probably been shaped over many centuries by grazing animals. It provides opportunities to see and hear bird species that prefer thick gorse cover with open areas studded by granite outcrops and surrounded by bell heather, ling and western gorse. A single gorse tip may provide a singing post for a Dartford warbler, an observation platform for stonechat or meadow pipit and, perhaps, a resting place for a rosy-breasted male linnet whose mate may be close by, sitting eggs.

It is a habitat over which kestrels hover and ravens tumble; a place where the opportunist characteristics of carrion crow and magpie will take full advantage of an ill-sited nest.

Dry grassland, a mixture of scrub, tussock grasses and rabbit-clipped turf, is set further inland, away from the salt-misted air of winter storms. It is a place where skylarks climb and sing; where lapwings lay their beautifully camouflaged eggs and where sparrowhawks ambush gathering flocks of small birds in spring and autumn.

The birds of maritime heath and dry grassland should include:

Kestrel

Latin name: *Falco tinnunculus*
Habitat: All areas though best seen in open landscapes
Food: Small mammals and birds / lizards /earthworms / insects
Islands status:
Resident A/G/H/ J/S

Kestrels are the most common bird of prey in the Channel Islands and can often be seen hovering in the wind above open heath, road-side verges, fields and cliffs before pouncing on their prey from above. Favourite nesting sites include cliff crevices, trees and quarry ledges. It is worth noting that, in general, if the bird hovers it is a kestrel.

Dartford warbler

Latin name: *Sylvia undata*
Habitat: Heath and commons
Food: insects / spiders
Islands status: Resident A/G/J

In spring, on a calm day, heathland is the ideal place to catch a glimpse of these delightful resident warblers. Thick gorse provides protection and warmth and only in spring, when the males sing from gorse spikes, is it possible to see them clearly. Dartford warblers are active birds but use gorse bushes as cover to great effect during their short dipping flights.

Stonechat

Latin name: *Saxicola torquata*
Habitat: Heath / dry grassland near coasts
Food: Mostly insects
Islands status: Resident A/G/J – Summer visitor S

Stonechats are rarely seen far from the coast. They enjoy a gorse and heathland habitat where they often perch on the very tip of a gorse spike or fence post. Male birds are about the same size as the robin but their black head, white collar and orange-red breast make them unmistakable.

Skylark

Latin name: *Alauda arvensis*
Habitat: Heath / dry grassland / dunes
Food: Insects / worms / seeds
Islands status: Resident A/G/J/S

Among the islands skylarks are dependent on
heathland, coastal dunes and commons. Where
these areas are subject to constant human impact, the
birds' numbers have declined considerably. They nest
and feed on the ground where much time is spent
searching for seeds, insects, spiders, worms and other
invertebrates. Their earthy colours provide superb
camouflage and their cascading song, used to establish
territory and attract a mate, is unmistakable.

Meadow pipit

Latin name: *Anthus pratensis*
Habitat: Heath / dry grassland / dunes
Food: Insects / seeds
Islands status: Resident A/G/J/S

A rather drab-coloured resident and a relative of
the wagtails, meadow pipit are a common Channel
Islands species. They are ground-dwelling birds,
frequently becoming host to young cuckoos
and prey to kestrels and sparrowhawks.

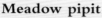

Linnet

Latin name: *Carduelis cannabina*
Habitat: Heath / dry grassland / dunes
Food: Insects / seeds
Islands status: Summer visitor G/H/J/A/S –
a few winter in all islands

Linnets are birds of heathland and hillside gorse.
The male is crimson-breasted, which distinguishes
it from the less colourful female. In spring and
summer they often fly in pairs and regularly use the
same perch near the nest site. They feed on seeds and
insects and can raise two or three broods each year.

Goldfinch

Latin name: *Carduelis carduelis*
Habitat: Heath / dunes / dry grass and scrubland / parks and gardens
Food: Insects / seeds
Islands status: Resident A/G/J – summer visitor S

Yellow, red, black, soft browns and white make goldfinches a splendid sight at any time of year but especially when seen in late summer feeding on thistles. Their musical twittering song can often be heard just before they descend on a thistle patch. The thistledown is cut neatly away by a perfectly designed bill and sent floating gently down the wind.

Lapwing

Latin name: *Vanellus vanellus*
Habitat: Coasts in winter / dry grassland and wet meadows (summer)
Food: Larval invertebrates / worms
Islands status: Scarce resident J
Winter visitor A/G/J/S

Lapwings are best seen in winter, especially when severe weather conditions prevail on the European mainland. At such times they have been known to descend on the islands in many thousands seeking unfrozen feeding grounds. During winter lapwings can usually be seen roosting close to the flood margins in open fields.

Cuckoo

Latin name: *Cuculus canorus*
Habitat: Heath / marshes / woodland
Food: Larval invertebrates / worms
Islands status: Summer visitor A/G/J/S

Cuckoos are summer Channel Island residents, usually arriving in mid to late April. Their song reflects their name but many early reports of the first cuckoo are confused with the call of the collared dove. They are brood parasites, laying a single egg in the nests of other bird. Some 50 species have played host to cuckoos. One cuckoo can lay between 15 and 25 eggs each season.

Wheatear

Latin name: *Oenanthe oenanthe*
Habitat: Coastal strip / shingle beaches / heath with short-cropped grass
Food: Insects and larvae / spiders / ants
Islands status: Summer migrant A/G/H/J/S

Although a few pairs of wheatears are occasionally recorded nesting in the islands, most of the spring arrivals are passage migrants heading north from tropical Africa. They prefer coastal margins when they first arrive in March, feeding along seawalls and rocky areas where piled vraic, warmed by the sun, produces flies and sand-hoppers. Male and female both have a white rump easily seen when in flight.

Short–eared owl

Latin name:
Asio flammeus
Habitat: Heath / marshes / sand dunes / arable land in winter
Food: Most small mammals, including rats and small rabbits
Islands status: Rare winter visitor A/G/J/S

Although not residents, short-eared owls are reported most years, usually in autumn, hunting in daytime over heaths. They are pale brown with long, elegant wings and a buoyant flight pattern. They present by far the best opportunity to study hunting owls.

Habitat 2
Cliffs and offshore islets

Steep, rugged cliffs and exposed offshore islets attract breeding birds used to a harsh environment. In fact most seabird species will spend two-thirds of their lives at sea, returning to land only during the breeding season. The fulmar, a true oceanic species, spends the first ten years of its life at sea before returning to land, often travelling thousands of miles to reach the cliff face on which it fledged.

Nest sites on cliffs and stacks vary according to species ranging from precarious ledges to caves, tussock grass to bare rock and crevices. Species nesting in exposed areas, such as herring gulls, will choose sites sheltered from the prevailing wind. Gannets, on the other hand, site nests wherever space is available within the colony.

Cliff paths around the islands provide perfect viewing platforms for watching these highly specialised summer breeding species. For maximum enjoyment, find a comfortable and safe place to sit and watch. Only then will the well camouflaged peregrine reveal itself by flying from a ledge or a razorbill's fast wing beats be seen heading in from the sea.

Shag

Latin name: *Phalacrocorax aristotelis*
Habitat: Cliffs / offshore reefs and islets
Food: Fish
Islands status: Resident: A/G/H/J/S

Shags are a common resident along coastal cliffs and inshore waters. During the breeding season colonies of nesting birds can be found in all coastal areas where cliffs and offshore stacks are present. Shags can often be seen in great numbers flying low over the water in long chain–like flocks, while travelling to and from feeding grounds. In colour they appear black but close observation, in good light, reveals a bottle green plumage. The diet consists entirely of fish and they are never seen on inland waters.

Cormorant

Latin name: *Phalacrocorax carbo*
Habitat: Offshore islets / inland cliff faces near fresh water
Food: Fish
Islands status: Resident: A/G/H/J/S

Similar to the shag, though a larger and much heavier bird, the cormorant prefers offshore islets and colonies have been recorded on Les Échréhous and the Maisons, three substantial islets among Les Minquiers reef. In recent years numbers seem to have increased substantially. Cormorants, unlike shags, will happily fish freshwater ponds, lakes and reservoirs. White cheeks at all times and a white patch on the thigh during the breeding season distinguish the cormorant from the shag.

Herring gull

Latin name: *Larus argentatus*
Habitat: Widespread, though cliffs /
offshore reefs and islets / rooftops
Food: Fish / shellfish / offal / refuse / eggs
Islands status: Resident: A/G/J/S

The herring gull is a common resident throughout
the islands. Although traditionally they prefer
grass-covered cliff slopes, and substantial ledges,
over recent years the species has spread from its traditional cliff breeding
grounds to rooftop sites in Jersey, especially where buildings are in close
proximity to the coast. Adult birds are pale blue-grey above and pure white
below with black tipped primary feathers. A thick, powerful yellow bill with
a red spot near to the tip (more prominent during the breeding season) and
pink legs are identifying features. Male and female are alike.

Great black-backed gull

Latin name: *Larus marinus*
Habitat: Cliffs / offshore reefs and islets /
occasionally rooftops
Food: All types of carrion / eggs / crustaceans /
worms / molluscs
Islands status: Resident: A/G/J/S

Great black-backed gulls are
found around all the island
coasts. During the breeding
season they nest with herring gull colonies on
coastal cliffs, usually building their own nests
slightly above the herring gulls and
producing young earlier. This enables them
to take advantage of herring gull eggs and
chicks as a food source for their own brood.
The great black-backed gull is the largest of
all the gulls seen in the Channel Islands,
whether visitor or resident. The upper wings
are black, edged with white. The bill is
yellow with a red patch at the tip of the
lower mandible and the legs are pink.

Lesser black-backed gull

Latin name: *Larus fuscus*
Habitat: Cliffs / offshore reefs and islets / occasionally rooftops
Food: Fish / eggs / crustaceans / worms / molluscs
Islands status: Resident: A/G/H/J/S

Although many Lesser black-backed gulls migrate south during the
winter months, some do winter in the Channel Islands. Head, breast
and under-parts are pure white, the heavy bill is yellow
with a reddish patch at the tip of the lower mandible and
the legs are yellow compared with the pink legs of the great black-backed gull.

Fulmar

Latin name: *Fulmarus glacialis*
Habitat: Cliffs / offshore reefs and islets
Food: Fish / eggs / crustaceans /
worms / molluscs
Islands status: Summer resident: A/G/J/S

A walk along cliff footpaths will usually reveal these
stiff-winged, barrel shaped birds, gliding on the warm updrafts of air along the
cliff faces or forming 'rafts' of roosting birds well out to sea. The fulmar is a
member of the tube-nose family and the tubes on the rather short yellow bill
are clearly seen on close observation. The wings, back and tail are grey
with primary feathers slightly darker. All other parts are white.

Puffin

Latin name: *Fratercula arctica*
Habitat: Cliffs and offshore islands where
earth burrows can be made
Food: Fish – usually sandeels in the Channel Islands
Islands status: Uncommon summer
resident: A/G/H/J/S

The puffin is one of the best-loved coastal species despite
numbers of summer breeding birds being comparatively low
throughout the islands compared with the huge colonies found
in northern Britain. Puffins nest in earth borrows in often
inaccessible cliff areas or on offshore islands where
disturbance during the breeding season is minimal.
They feed on fish – sandeels in particular – and
occasionally crustaceans and molluscs.

Razorbill

Latin name: *Alca torda*
Habitat: Cliffs and offshore islands
Food: Fish / molluscs / crustaceans
Islands status: Rare breeding visitor A/G/H/J/S

The razorbill is an upright black and white bird with a thick, square bill featuring a thin white line at the tip. A single egg is laid on a narrow rocky ledge. Nature has designed the egg in a rather pointed pear-shape which helps prevent it from rolling off the ledge. Food consists of fish, molluscs and crustaceans. Like the puffin, the razorbill dives for its food and hunting can take place in depths of up to 55 metres.

Guillemot

Latin name: *Uria aalge*
Habitat: Cliffs and offshore stacks
Food: Fish / molluscs / crustaceans
Islands status: A/S breeding species. G/J winter visitor

Guillemots are a fairly common breeding species on the rugged cliff faces of Alderney and Sark where nest sites are inaccessible. In the rest of the islands they are regarded as uncommon visitors at most times of the year. They are a truly marine species, coming ashore only to breed. The head, neck and back are dark brown; underparts are white and there is a thin white wing bar. They plunge dive when feeding and have been recorded at depths of up to 400 ft.

Stock dove

Latin name: *Columba oenas*
Habitat: Cliff caves / rock crevices / tree holes
Food: Seeds / grain / clover / plant shoots
Islands status: Resident G/J – Occasional visitor
A – Very rare S

The stock dove's general appearance is that of a blue-grey pigeon with dark flight feathers. Outside the breeding season they will often feed in flocks on grassland or ploughed and fallow fields. They breed in rock crevices and caves on cliffs and occasionally in tree holes.

Peregrine falcon

Latin name:

Falco peregrinus

Habitat: Sheltered cliff face
ledges / offshore islets

Food: Birds

Islands status: Rare resident
A/G/H/J/S

Peregrine falcons seem to prefer a
coastal habitat where waders and cliff-
dwelling birds are numerous.
Roosts include large offshore
reefs and buildings. When
prey is marked, the falcon
dives with almost closed
wings at incredible speed
(estimates suggest between 100–
200 mph). A rather thick set falcon, the
peregrine is slate-grey above and creamy-white
below with heavy black barring across the breast and underparts. A close
view shows moustachial streaks and a white throat. The wings are distinctly
pointed and the tail rather short.

Raven

Latin name: *Corvus corax*

Habitat: Cliff face ledges /
offshore islets

Food: Rabbit carcasses / bird
eggs and young / reptiles /
small mammals / fish offal

Islands status: Resident
A/G/J/S

Although occasionally seen
over-flying rural parts of the
islands, ravens are specifically a
coastal breeding species here,
preferring to nest on steep rocky crags in exposed cliff areas. The very size of
this largest of British crows separates it from other species. In appearance it is
all black with a powerful bill and longish neck. The flight feathers are often
splayed, finger-like, and the tail is wedge-shaped and rather rounded.

Swift

Latin name: *Apus apus*
Habitat: Crevices in cliffs, stone walls and roof eves
Food: Flying insects
Islands status: Summer visitor A/G/J/S

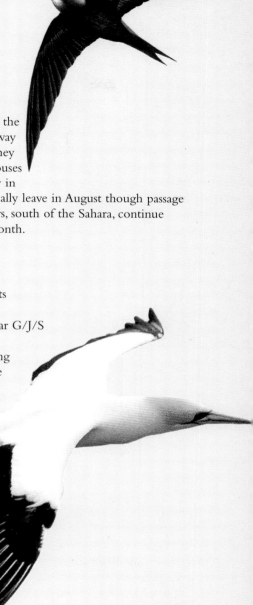

From the end of April swifts pass through the islands in considerable numbers on their way north, though many stay to breed here. They nest in rock crevices, under the eves of houses and in holes where mortar has worn away in granite piers and walls. Breeding birds usually leave in August though passage migrants returning to their winter quarters, south of the Sahara, continue passing through the island for at least a month.

Gannet

Latin name: *Morus bassanus*
Habitat: Offshore stacks / substantial islets
Food: Fish
Islands status: Breeding A offshore all year G/J/S

The gannet can occasionally be seen fishing well offshore in all island waters. There are substantial breeding colonies sited close to Alderney and others on the western coast of France. The gannet's hunting technique is dramatic and usually identifies the bird at distance. After marking a fish, the gannet will plunge head first into the water in chase. The bill is grey and dagger-like and the head pale yellow. The body is white and the wing tips black. Food consists of a variety of mid-water and surface fishes.

Habitat 3
The tide line

Despite their comparatively small size, the islands support a considerable diversity of bird species associated with the wild, intertidal zone. In calm weather, as the tide surges in, rocky outcrops beyond the reach of the sea are often crowded with redshank, dunlin, sanderling, the occasional pure white plumage of little egrets and the hunched forms of grey herons.

There is a magical atmosphere about the coastline in winter but the sight and sound is not just that of wading birds. Out among the offshore reefs look for small flocks of red-breasted mergansers feeding in the shallows and sharing the habitat with great-crested grebes and resident shags.

A few miles off the coast there are migration routes used by hundreds of thousands of sea birds that one would not normally connect with the Island – kittiwakes, skewers, eider duck, little gulls and scoters. Every year many of these birds are noted and counted, with the help of sophisticated telescopes, by local bird recorders.

Brent goose

Latin name: *Branta bernicla*
Habitat: Tidal shores / protected bays
Food: Eel grass / green algae
Islands status: Winter migrant G/J
Rare winter visitors A/S

Brent geese begin arriving among the islands from their Siberian Arctic breeding grounds from late September, with numbers building throughout the month of October. In Jersey, numbers range from 800 to 1,500 birds, depending largely on the success of the breeding season. The Brent is the smallest of the British geese, not much bigger than the mallard. Their general appearance is black beneath and dark brown above. They feed on eel grass beds (Zostera marina) uncovered by the tide and occasionally on inland pastures during harsh weather.

Curlew

Latin name: *Numenius arquata*
Habitat: Tidal shores / mudflats /
occasionally on inland pastures
Food: Worms / small molluscs / crustaceans
Islands status: Winter visitor A/G/H/J/S

The curlew is a rather large brown bird with a long, down-curved bill and a white back and rump. They frequent both rocky and sandy shores and roost on offshore reefs. Curlews spend the autumn and winter among the islands, feeding on lugworms, small molluscs, crustaceans and occasionally fish. The curlew is the largest of the British wading birds.

Bar-tailed godwit

Winter

Latin name: *Limosa lapponica*
Habitat: Tidal shores / mudflats
Food: Worms / small molluscs / crustaceans
Islands status: Winter visitor A/G/J

In winter, when we are most likely to see them, bar-tailed godwits are greyish brown above and buff-white below. The slightly up-curved, long and slender bill is flesh coloured, and the legs, compared with other, larger waders, are rather short. There is a prominent white rump best seen in flight and, unlike the black-tailed godwit, there is no white on the wings. As the name indicates, the tail, not always easy to see in the field, is finely barred. The bar-tail is a winter visitor to our coasts and is very rarely seen inland. They are a gregarious species mixing happily with other waders on beaches and mudflats.

Oystercatcher

Latin name: *Haematopus ostralegus*
Habitat: Tidal shores / mudflats / reefs and rocky coasts
Food: Mussels / cockles / worms
Islands status: Resident A/G/J/S

Oystercatchers breed throughout the Channel Islands but
numbers present increase substantially in the autumn
when many hundreds of British and Scandinavian birds
arrive to spend the winter here. Those birds which do breed
among the islands lay their eggs on bare granite ledges and stony
beaches with no nest material. The eggs are beautifully camouflaged.

Redshank

Latin name: *Tringa totanus*
Habitat: Tidal shores / mudflats / offhore reefs
Food: Worms / small crustaceans
Islands status: Winter visitor A/G/J – Occasional winter S

Redshanks are regular visitors. They arrive in autumn and remain
until March and early April. Often seen among the smaller waders on
the tide line, the bird has bright red legs which are easily seen
even at a considerable distance. The general colour in winter is grey-
brown above and rather paler below. Their winter diet consists of worms,
molluscs and tiny crustaceans which they take from the sand with a slender
red bill, tipped with black.

Turnstone

Winter

Latin name: *Arenaria interpres*
Habitat: Tidal shores / rocky gullies / stony areas
Food: Small crustaceans / marine invertebrates
Islands status: Winter visitor A/G/J/S

Turnstones are winter visitors and during the cold months the islands
plays host to a significant part of the European population. Often,
when birds arrive in early autumn, they are still in breeding plumage but the
beautiful chestnut and tortoiseshell brown upper parts become rather drab
brown as winter progresses. Although they do feed on open sand they spend
much of their time in rocky gullies and stony areas where there are molluscs,
crustaceans and sand hoppers. Roosting flocks can often be seen on shingle
banks above the high tide mark.

Grey plover

Winter

Latin name: *Pluvialis squatarola*
Habitat: Sandy shores / mud flats
Food: Small crustaceans / worms
Islands status: Winter visitor A/G/J

Grey plovers are birds of the Arctic tundra but when they
arrive in the islands during autumn they become shore birds. They seldom
gather in flocks unless roosting on offshore reefs. More often they are solitary
birds seen on the middle shore and down to the lowest tide line. In
appearance they are a grey, plover-like wader with a white rump, longish
black legs and a rather short black bill. In flight, the underwing shows a
distinctive black patch.

Ringed plover

Winter

Latin name: *Charadrius hiaticula*
Habitat: Sandy shores / stony beaches
Food: Small crustaceans / worms
Islands status: Winter visitor A/G/H/J – Occasional S

Small flocks of ringed plovers arrive during autumn and remain
until March or April. Their winter plumage is greyish-brown above
and white below with a dark, almost black, band around the upper
breast. The short bill is orange, tipped with black and the legs, too, are
orange. In flight the ringed plover shows strong white wing bars. On the
ground it appears as a rather small, dumpy bird, although when feeding on
flat sandy shores it moves extremely quickly, usually in short running bursts.

Sanderling

Winter

Latin name: *Calidris alba*
Habitat: Sandy shores
Food: small shrimps
Islands status: Winter visitor G/J – Autumn and
winter migrant A

Small flocks of sanderling spend the winter months feeding
along sandy and muddy shores. They are easily distinguished
by their overall pale appearance – pale grey above, white below. The
bill and legs are black and there is a dark smudge at the bend of the wing.
Sanderlings are active birds, spending much of their feeding time on the run at
the edge of the tide. They are often seen feeding with dunlin and, because of the
contrasting colour comparisons this is a good time to separate the two species.

Dunlin

Latin name: *Calidris alpina*
Habitat: Sandy shores
Food: Invertebrates
Islands status: Winter visitor A/G/J

The dunlin is probably the most common of the small
wintering waders. In appearance it is much darker than the sanderling. Upper
parts are a greyish brown, lower parts a creamy white with some streaking on the
breast. The bill and legs are dark. In summer they are birds of moorland and Arctic
tundra and it is estimated that well over a million dunlin winter on British coasts.

Purple sandpiper

Latin name: *Calidris maritima*
Habitat: Rocky coasts / offshore reefs
Food: Small marine worms
Islands status: Winter visitor
A/G/J – Occasional winter S

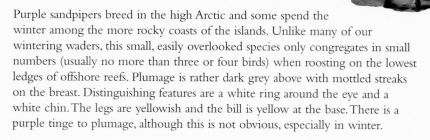

Purple sandpipers breed in the high Arctic and some spend the
winter among the more rocky coasts of the islands. Unlike many of our
wintering waders, this small, easily overlooked species only congregates in small
numbers (usually no more than three or four birds) when roosting on the lowest
ledges of offshore reefs. Plumage is rather dark grey above with mottled streaks
on the breast. Distinguishing features are a white ring around the eye and a
white chin. The legs are yellowish and the bill is yellow at the base. There is a
purple tinge to plumage, although this is not obvious, especially in winter.

Rock pipit

Latin name: *Anthus spinoletta petrosus*
Habitat: Rocky coasts / offshore reefs / splash zone
Food: Insects / tiny crustaceans
Islands status: Resident A/G/J/S

The rock pipit is resident throughout the islands. A
member of the wagtail family, it is found almost
exclusively on rocky seashores, cliffs and beaches. The back is a dark, olive-
brown tinged with grey. Underparts are a light greyish buff streaked with
black. The outer tail feathers are an off-white and the dark, almost black legs
help distinguish it from other pipits. The rock pipit feeds on sand flies and
other insects, sand hoppers and tiny crustaceans. Occasionally, seeds are
included in their diet.

Little egret

Latin name: *Egretta garzetta*
Habitat: Rocky intertidal beaches / offshore reefs
Food: Mainly fish / prawns / shrimps
Islands status: Resident breeding species
J – winter visitor A/G/S

The gradual spread north of these elegant, white, heron-like birds has made them a regular winter feature. They are present from early autumn until spring in varying numbers. If weather and tide allow, little egrets roost on the larger offshore reefs close to their feeding grounds. During spring tides and gales they will move inland to more protected roosts. They are perhaps the easiest of our shore birds to identify with their elegantly curved neck, all-white plumage, long, slender black bill, black legs and yellow feet.

Kingfisher

Latin name: *Alcedo atthis*
Habitat: Rocky coasts / rock pools / all types of fresh water
Food: Fish
Islands status: Winter Visitor A/G/J

The kingfisher is mainly a winter visitor, with only an occasional pair staying to breed. Brightly coloured and instantly recognised, the species is more often seen on the coast than inland, especially during the winter months. Any area that affords ledges from which kingfishers can dive for small fish is a good place to see them. The crevices in harbour walls and piers, pontoons, inshore reefs and even mooring ropes provide excellent hunting platforms for kingfishers.

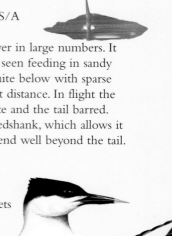

Greenshank

Latin name: *Tringa nebularia*
Habitat: Beaches / sandy shallows / rock pools
Food: Worms / fish
Islands status: Winter visitor J – Scarce migrant G/S/A

The greenshank is a regular winter visitor, though never in large numbers. It is perhaps the most elegant of the shore waders, often seen feeding in sandy rock pools. The greenshank is dark grey above and white below with sparse streaking on the breast. The bill is dark, almost black at distance. In flight the rump, which extends in a V shape up the back, is white and the tail barred. The dark legs are distinctly longer than those of the redshank, which allows it to feed in quite deep pools. During flight the legs extend well beyond the tail.

Sandwich tern

Latin name: *Sterna sandvicensis*
Habitat: Inshore rocky coasts / offshore reefs and islets
Food: Small fish
Islands status: Spring and autumn
migrants A/G/J/S

The sandwich tern is pale grey above and white beneath and in breeding plumage there is a full black cap extending to the nape and terminating in a short ragged crest. The bill is black with a yellow tip although this is difficult to make out at distance. The harsh, ratchetty, chattering voice is usually the first thing that draws attention to their presence. With the typical buoyant flight of the terns they hunt small fish by hovering and plunging.

Common tern

Latin name: *Sterna hirundo*
Habitat: Breeds on small islets
around the Channel Islands
Food: Worms / fish
Islands status: Summer migrants A/G/J/S

The common tern is an elegant seabird, pale grey above and white below. Like other terns, it has a velvet black cap and the bill is red, tipped with black. The tail is forked with swallow-like outer tail feathers. When seen fishing the high tide close inshore, common terns plunge headfirst into the sea in pursuit of small fish.

Red-breasted merganser

Latin name:
Mergus serrator
Habitat:
Inshore rocky coasts
Food: Fish
Islands status: Winter
visitor A/G/J

The red-breasted merganser is a winter visitor, preferring the rocky offshore shallows and protected bays where it hunts for small fish. Flocks of several dozen birds (often referred to as 'rafts') and individuals can be seen from autumn through to spring. During very rough weather birds will often hunt close in shore. Red-breasted mergansers are saw-billed ducks hence the Latin, serrator. The bill is finely serrated in order to grip small fish.

Great-crested grebe

Latin name: *Podiceps cristatus*
Habitat: Inshore rocky coasts
Food: Fish / molluscs / crustaceans
Islands status: Winter migrant and visitor A/G/J

The great-crested grebe is a winter visitor and when they arrive here they are normally pale grey and white with a long slender neck and pointed bill. They are seen frequently fishing in protected bays and further offshore during calmer weather. Although mostly a maritime species here in its winter quarters, individual birds can occasionally be seen fishing fresh water inland.

Winter

Habitat 4
Woodlands

Most woodland habitats in the Channel Islands are set in steep-sided valleys protected from strong winter gales. They are usually a mixture of deciduous trees, accompanied by a diversity of under-storey shrubs and wild flora. In such a habitat, knowledge of bird song and contact calls is always an advantage because lush vegetation and the thick summer growth of the upper canopy provide excellent cover for birds.

Early morning, when most birds are intent on feeding, is probably the best time of day to see the woodland species. The song of a blackcap, collared dove or chiffchaff will inevitably suggest there are birds present despite the quiet atmosphere that often envelopes woodlands during the heat of the day.

The best advice for woodland bird watching is to sit quietly on a bank or tree stump at the edge of a sunny glade and wait and watch. As peace returns birds will begin to move more confidently.

Jay

Latin name: *Glandarius garrulus*
Habitat: Woodland / parkland
Food: Acorns / fruit / berries
Islands status: Resident J – Rarely
recorded A/G/H/S

This colourful member of
the crow family was
introduced into Jersey in or
around 1875 and is now regarded as a common
resident. Only four sightings have been recorded
in Guernsey and six in Alderney, the last in
1937 and 1987 respectively.
In appearance jays are pinkish brown
with distinctive blue and white wing
panels. They are easily disturbed and
are usually noticed flying away,
when the distinctive black tail and
white rump can best be seen.

Great spotted
woodpecker

Latin name: *Dendrocopos major*
Habitat: Woodland / parkland
Food: Insects / seeds / grubs
Islands status: Resident J –
Rarely recorded A/G/H/S

Great spotted woodpeckers were
first found breeding in Jersey in
1952 in Rosel Manor woods and are
Jersey's only resident woodpeckers.
Now they can be found in many of
the island's woodland valleys and in
winter often visit garden bird tables
close to woodland fringes. They are
starling-sized birds with distinctive red,
white and black plumage and the male has
a bright red patch on the neck.

♂

Sparrowhawk

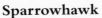

Latin name: *Accipiter nisus*
Habitat: Woodland / Farmland
with hedgerows
Food: Small birds taken on the wing
Islands status: Resident G/J/A –
Rarely recorded H/S

Sparrowhawks are quite common in
Guernsey and Jersey and are seen
regularly in Alderney. They use
regular feeding stations such as tree
stumps and fence posts where
scattered feathers are an excellent
indication of their presence.
Distinguishing
markings include
strongly barred
underparts and a
white stripe above
the eye. Sparrowhawks do
not hover.

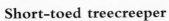

Short-toed treecreeper

Latin name: *Certhia brachydactyla*
Habitat: Woodland / parks
Food: Insects
Islands status: Resident G/J – Rarely recorded A/H/S

Short-toed treecreepers are tiny, mouse-like birds
found in woodland areas. As the name suggests, they
climb from the base of a tree in a steady upward spiral
searching for insects in the bark crevices. They will
then fly down to the base of the next tree and begin
the feeding process again. Short-toed treecreepers are
well-camouflaged birds, streaked with buffs and browns
above and white below.

Great tit

Latin name: *Parus major*
Habitat: Woodland / parks / gardens
Food: Insects / seeds / fruit
Islands status: Resident G/A/J/S

A common resident in all the Channel Islands, great tits are
distinguished from other titmice by their relatively large
size, black head, white cheeks and bright yellow breast
with a central wide black vertical line. Although essentially woodland birds,
great tits are easily encouraged to use nest boxes in mature gardens. They are
best seen at the garden bird table during the winter months.

Blue tit

Latin name: *Parus caeruleus*
Habitat: Woodland / parks / gardens
Food: Insects and larvae / seeds / fruit
Islands status: Resident G/A/J/S

Blue tits are amongst the islands' most colourful
resident birds and are common in woodlands where their
preferred nesting tree is the oak. Their natural food is insects,
larvae, spiders and centipedes, with occasional fruit and seeds,
although coconut, peanuts and fat from the winter bird table have widened
their diet considerably.

Chiffchaff

Latin name: *Phylloscopus collybitus*
Habitat: Woodland
Food: Insects and larvae
Islands status: Summer resident G/A/J/S. Some
winter A/G/J

The chiffchaff, like the cuckoo, is one of the few birds named
after its song. In appearance it is so like the willow warbler
that it takes an expert to separate the two in the field. For the
casual observer, recognition must come from the song. A small
number of chiffchaffs remain among the islands during the winter months
and in spring the local population is augmented by migrants from the south.

Bullfinch

Latin name: *Pyrrhula pyrrhula*
Habitat: Woodland margins / open parkland
Food: Berries / buds / seeds
Islands status: Resident G/J. Uncommon resident A/S

Bullfinch numbers can be deceptive because of their
secretive nature. Despite the male's grey back, jet-
black head, and rose-pink breast, in dense thickets they can be very
difficult to see. A good recognition feature is the snow-white rump – often the
only glimpse obtained of the bird as it flies away. Due to their taste for fruit
tree buds they are unwelcome in orchard areas.

Blackcap

Latin name: *Sylvia atricapilla*
Habitat: Woodland / parkland / gardens
Food: Insects / larvae / berries
Islands status: Resident J. Summer visitor G/A/S

Blackcaps are probably the easiest resident warblers to
recognise. A grey back and a velvet-black cap distinguishes
the male bird. The female has a browner back and brownish
ginger cap. Most blackcaps spend the winter in Africa and those
that remain in the islands sometimes suffer from severe
weather which can take its toll of this rather large warbler.
In late spring their song, often compared with that of the
nightingale, allows easy recognition.

Willow warbler

Latin name: *Phylloscopus trochilus*
Habitat: Woodland / parkland / gardens
Food: Insects / larvae
Islands status: Summer visitor A/G/J/S

Willow warblers, summer visitors to the islands, are superb
songsters. Although they are very similar to the chiffchaff
in appearance, the bird's cascading song clearly separates
the two species. They frequent all types of woodland
habitat and feed on insects and larvae. Many move
north through the islands during the spring
migration and in summer they are one of the
commonest birds in Europe.

Wren

Latin name: *Troglodytes troglodytes*
Habitat: Woodland / hedgerows / gardens
Food: Insects / spiders
Islands status: Resident A/G/J/S

The wren's scientific name, Troglodytes troglodytes, means 'cave dweller' and, although the bird's habitat is dark and rather gloomy woodland thickets, deep hedgerows and briar patches – a very cavy atmosphere – it is more likely that the name comes from the dark, round entrance to its nest. Wrens are one of the most common birds and their loud and vigorous song belies the fact that they are also one of the smallest. They are one of the few British species which build a roofed nest.

Mistle thrush

Latin name: *Turdus viscivorus*
Habitat: Woodland / hedgerows / parkland
Food: Insects / fruit / berries
Islands status: Uncommon resident G/J. Scarce visitor A/S

Active pairs of mistle thrushes can be seen gathering nest material among fallow fields as early as February. They are the largest of the thrush family and the earliest of Jersey's song birds to breed. The nest, usually somewhat exposed, is built from roots and grasses in the fork of a tree. They are very upright birds on the ground and their characteristically vigorous, somewhat blackbird-like song is often heard during stormy weather, hence one of its vernacular names, storm-cock.

Goldcrest

Latin name: *Regulus regulus*
Habitat: Woodland / hedgerows / parks / gardens
Food: Small insects
Islands status: Resident G/J Winter visitor A/S

The goldcrest is Britain's smallest bird, only nine centimetres long and weighing the equivalent of a five-pence piece. The species favour conifers but seem perfectly content in mixed woodlands, parks and gardens where single firs can often be found. Resident birds are joined by migrants from Scandinavia during the autumn and winter and it is astonishing that these diminutive birds manage to make such long migrations over open sea twice a year.

Spotted flycatcher

Latin name: *Muscicapa striata*
Habitat: Woodland margins / hedgerows / parks / gardens
Food: Flying insects
Islands status: Summer visitor G/J/A/S

So dependent are spotted flycatchers on insects that they are the last of
the summer migrants to arrive in the islands. They prefer woodland
margins and will repeatedly use the same branch from which to hunt a
variety of flying insects, from butterflies to wasps. Overhanging banks, ivy
and overgrown garden trellises are among their favourite nesting sites, and
open-fronted nest boxes placed in well-covered garden areas will encourage
them to take up residence. Their winter quarters are in Africa.

Long-tailed tit

Latin name: *Aegithalos caudatus*
Habitat: Woodland margins /
hedgerows / parks / gardens
Food: Flying insects
Islands status: Resident G/J. Rare migrant A/S

The long-tailed tit has been described as a flying
teaspoon and as flocks, sometimes forty or fifty
strong, pass overhead among woodland trees or thick hedgerows, the reason
for that description becomes clear. Their nest, which can take several weeks
to build, is a delightful oval structure of cobwebs, mosses and lichens lined
with hundreds of small feathers. The adults often brood at the same time
and the female lays up to twelve eggs.

Long-eared owl

Latin name: *Asio otus*
Habitat: Woodland / copses / plantations
Food: Voles and other small mammals
Islands status: Resident in Guernsey,
Jersey and Herm G/J/A/S
(has bred in Jersey)

Long-eared owls are migratory birds. Usually quite scarce,
they appear to be recorded more frequently during snowy
weather. The long ear tufts are diagnostic.
Two pairs nested and raised young in Jersey during 2004

Habitat 5
Freshwater wetlands

Wetlands are among the most fascinating habitats, possibly
because although many of the species may change as winter
progresses into spring and summer, reed beds, open water,
marshes and wet meadows always seem to contain active bird life.
In winter, when naturally marshy ground begins to saturate and form still
water patches, look for snipe, teal and shoveler duck. Moorhens will be less
secretive at this time of year, sharing the open glaze of flood water with
resident mallard, tufted duck and coot. Look for visiting waders too –
common sandpiper, roosting greenshanks, grey herons and perhaps even the
occasional water pipit in autumn.
As spring progresses and the water level drops, farmers will often allow cattle
to graze wet meadows and, as their feet disturb insects among the grasses
yellow wagtails will often take full advantage of the feast. Certainly swallows,
house martins and swifts will use this and other wetlands to full advantage as
the warm weather encourages millions of flying insects to hatch.
The songs of summer visitors, whitethroats, reed and sedge warblers, all
newly arrived from Africa, will join the resident Cetti's warblers among
yellow flag iris and reed margins. Whatever the time of year, wetlands provide
some fascinating birdwatching.

Grey heron

Latin name: *Ardea cinerea*
Habitat: Inshore rocky coasts / wetlands
Food: Fish / frogs / small mammals / occasionally birds
Islands status: Winter visitor and migrant A/G/J/S

Grey herons are mostly winter visitors to the islands. Although some stay during the summer months they do not breed here. From autumn through to spring they feed among low-tide rock pools and gullies and will hunt inland wetland areas – reservoirs, natural ponds, small streams, marshes and ornamental ponds. Their diet includes fish, small mammals, birds and frogs.

Mallard

Latin name: *Anas platyrhinchos*
Habitat: Ponds / lakes / reservoirs / small streams
Food: Varies
Islands status: Resident G/J/A/S

The mallard is the most common duck among the islands. They frequent most of wetlands, reservoirs, ornamental lakes and ponds, small harbours where fresh water emanates and along small streams. Mallards build their nests well away from water, usually on the ground in thick grassy cover and occasionally in trees and buildings.

Tufted duck

Latin name: Aythya fuligula
Habitat: Ponds / lakes /
reservoirs / small streams
Food: Varies
Islands status: Resident J – Rare
winter visitor and migrant G/A

Tufted ducks enjoy open freshwater and reservoirs and
large lakes are excellent places to see them. At one time only a winter visitor,
the tufted duck has been an established resident in Jersey since the 1970s and
is now widespread and fairly common. Although they have bred in Guernsey
they are more frequently seen as winter visitors. Migrants seen among the
islands are from Scandinavia and Russia.

Teal

Latin name: *Anas crecca*
Habitat: Shallow wetlands with cover
Food: Seeds / vegetable matter / invertebrates
Islands status: Winter visitor
and migrant G/J/A

Teal, winter visitors to the islands, are about one
third the size of mallard and are the smallest of our
wintering ducks. They feed on vegetable matter and small invertebrates in shallow
water covering a soft, muddy bottom. Marshes and the flooded margins of lakes
and ponds will often support small numbers each winter.

Shoveler

Latin name: *Anas clypeata*
Habitat: Open shallow water with cover
Food: Seeds / invertebrates
Islands status: Winter visitor and migrant
G/J – Occasionally recorded A

Small numbers of shovelers arrive among the islands in
winter although they are considered scarce winter visitors. The two sexes are
markedly different and, although there is a resemblance to the mallard, their
broad, shovel-like bill and the male's bright white front distinguishes them.
They feed on seeds and invertebrates suspended on or just below the surface
by sifting the water with their finely serrated bills.

Pochard

Latin name: *Aythya ferina*
Habitat: Open shallow water with cover
Food: Seeds / plant material
Islands status: Winter visitor and migrant G/J/A

Although regular winter visitors, pochards are by no means common. They frequent shallow water with thick vegetation around the margins where they dive for plant material and seeds. In recent years one or two pairs have occasionally remained to breed. The male, with its chestnut head and neck, black breast and pale grey back is easily recognised though the greys and browns of the female can cause identification problems especially when roosting. Both birds have a wide pale band around the centre of the black-tipped bill.

Coot

Latin name: *Fulica atra*
Habitat: Open shallow water with plenty of vegetation
Food: Seeds / plant material / insects / roots
Islands status: Resident and winter visitor G/J/A

Although regarded as a scarce breeding species in the islands, numbers are greatly increased by wintering birds. Coots are easily distinguished from the similar moorhen by their larger size and the white forehead shield and bill. They find their food by diving from the surface to depths of up to twenty feet in search of roots, reed shoots and water insects.

Moorhen

Latin name: *Gallinula chloropus*
Habitat: Open shallow water with plenty of vegetation
Food: Seeds / plant material / insects / insect larvae
Islands status: Resident G/J/A – Possible resident S

Moorhens are common residents in Guernsey and Jersey, less so in Alderney. They can be found on ponds, reservoirs and marshy ground where there is thick vegetation. They appear to be black but close observation will reveal a dark brown back with blackish underparts, the two colours separated by a thin white line. For quick identification, however, the red forehead shield and yellow tipped bill and the flicking white tail are distinctive. The winter population is augmented by migrants from the north.

Water rail

Latin name: *Rallus aquaticus*
Habitat: Reed beds / thick vegetation
Food: Seeds / insects /
insect larvae / berries
Islands status: Winter visitor and
migrant G/A/J/S

Water rails are winter visitors and
migrants to the islands and
although birds are occasionally
seen during the breeding season there is no
confirmed record of nesting. The muted browns and greys of
their plumage make these shy birds difficult to spot and the most frequent
guide to their presence is the shrill squeal of their call from dense vegetation.

Snipe

Latin name: *Gallinago gallinago*
Habitat: Freshwater margins / marshy areas
Food: Insects / insect larvae / worms
Islands status: Winter visitor and
migrant G/A/J/S

Snipe are fairly common winter visitors to most of the islands
and numbers increase during severe weather elsewhere.
They are beautifully camouflaged with streaks of warm
browns, buff and white and when at rest can be difficult
to locate.

Reed warbler

Latin name: *Acrocephalus scirpaceus*
Habitat: Reed beds
Food: Insects
Islands status: Summer visitors and migrants G/A/J –
Rare migrant S

Reed warblers are summer visitors to the islands, arriving
from mid–April. They build their nests among reeds over
shallow water using some old and some new stems as part of
the construction. This small warbler's plumage is in muted
shades of brown and buff and its lively chattering song is
part of the summer scene among reed beds.

Sedge warbler

Latin name: *Acrocephalus schoenobaenus*
Habitat: Reed beds
Food: Insects
Islands status: Summer visitor and migrant
G/A/J – Uncommon migrant S

Sedge warblers enjoy a reed-bed environment. Their streaked brown head and back, well-marked cream eye-stripe and necklace of dark spots on the throat make them easily distinguishable from reed warblers. Many sedge warblers pass through the island on their way north from their winter quarters, south of the Sahara, and some usually stay as summer residents.

Reed bunting

♂

Latin name: *Emberiza schoeniclus*
Habitat: Reed beds
Food: Seeds / insects / invertebrates
Islands status: Rare summer/common winter visitors G/J/A – Recorded S

The reed bunting is a bird of the reed beds but in other areas the species is expanding into drier habitats. In winter they can be seen among the flocks of mixed finches feeding in arable fields. The male is easily recognised by its black hood and bib separated by a white collar. The back is streaked with chestnut, black and brown. Females are streaked with browns, buff and black with a distinctive cream eyebrow and mustachial streak joining at the rear of the ear coverts.

♂

Bearded tit

Latin name: *Panurus biarmicus*
Habitat: Reed beds
Food: Insects summer / small seeds winter
Islands status: Resident J – Scarce winter visitor G. Recorded A

The preferred habitat of the bearded tit is dense reed beds and their food is insects in summer supplemented by small seeds in winter. Their distinctive gait when on the ground accounts for their regional name of red pheasant. Bearded tits can suffer badly during severe winter weather but recent records show that they have the ability to recover very quickly. Migration studies have shown there is movement between Jersey, Guernsey, England and the Netherlands.

Cetti's warbler

Latin name: *Cettia cetti*
Habitat: Reed beds
Food: Insects / spiders
Islands status: Resident G/J – Summer visitor S Recorded A

A somewhat secretive bird whose explosive song usually reveals its presence. The main features of the Cetti's warbler's plumage are warm brown upper parts, creamy white underparts, with a prominent pale streak above the eye and a rounded tail.

Common sandpiper

Latin name: *Actitis hypoleucos*
Habitat: Freshwater margins almost anywhere
Food: Invertebrates
Islands status: Spring and autumn migrant A/G/J/S

The islands are a staging post for the common sandpiper. Birds heading north to their breeding grounds pass through the islands in spring, and again in autumn when they return to their winter quarters in tropical Africa. Their most distinctive feature is a repeated bobbing action. Upper parts and breast are a warm brown, underparts are white and there is a clear, white stripe above the eye.

Marsh harrier

Latin name:
Circus aeruginosus
Habitat: Freshwater margins almost anywhere
Food: Birds / small mammals / frogs
Islands status: Breeds J – Spring and autumn migrant A/G/J – Recorded S

♀

Rarely a year goes by without marsh harriers visiting the major islands, coursing reed beds, rough grassland and heath. They fly with a flapping and gliding motion, the wings held in a shallow V-shape. Plumage differs considerably depending on age. The adult males are dark brown with a pale cream-coloured head and ash-grey tail. Females are larger birds and are distinguished by a more pronounced creamy-coloured crown, head and throat with pale creamy patches on the shoulders.

Habitat 6
Farmland, parks and gardens

This group of mixed and often overlapping habitats cover a wide variety of bird species, many of which will be regular garden visitors from autumn through to spring. The black-headed gull has been included because it is as likely to be seen following the plough, feeding among flooded fields or bathing on inland reservoirs as it is on the coast.

Starling

Latin name: *Sturnus vulgaris*
Habitat: Farmland / open parkland / suburbs / gardens
Food: Leatherjackets / insects / caterpillars / ants
Islands status: Resident G/A/J/S

The starling is probably the most familiar of all bird species, though numbers have halved over the past decade. They are nomadic birds and huge flocks frequently move freely around northern Europe and Great Britain. Although their plumage at first appears to be black, iridescent colours of red, purple, green and blue shine out when the bird is seen in good light. During the early summer their bills change from grey to yellow.

House sparrow

Latin name: *Passer domesticus*
Habitat: Close to human habitation
Food: Seeds / buds / varied in winter
Islands status: Resident G/A/J/S

Sparrows establish small nesting colonies under the eaves of houses, in holes in walls occasionally in hedgerows. They are extremely noisy during the breeding season when cock sparrows loudly advertise their newly made nests to any passing female. When weather conditions are suitable they will often raise as many as three broods during the season between April until late August.

Wood pigeon

Latin name: *Columba palumbus*
Habitat: Woodland fringes / parkland
Food: Fruit and berries /
cultivated brassicas / seeds
Islands status: Resident A/G/J/S

Wood pigeons spend much of their time feeding on the ground but roost and nest exclusively in trees. At a distance they appear grey but the breast is a delicate pink and, on adult birds, there is a white neck mark edged with green and pink. In flight their white wing-bars are conspicuous and, although appearing heavy on the ground, they are strong fliers. In winter the islands' population is considerably increased by large numbers of wintering birds.

Collared dove

Latin name: *Streptopelia decaocto*
Habitat: Parkland / farms / coniferous trees in suburbs
Food: Fruit / seeds / grain
Islands status: Resident G/A/J S

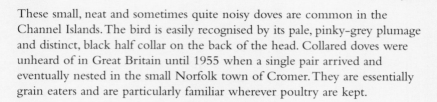

These small, neat and sometimes quite noisy doves are common in the Channel Islands. The bird is easily recognised by its pale, pinky-grey plumage and distinct, black half collar on the back of the head. Collared doves were unheard of in Great Britain until 1955 when a single pair arrived and eventually nested in the small Norfolk town of Cromer. They are essentially grain eaters and are particularly familiar wherever poultry are kept.

Dunnock

Latin name: *Prunella modularis*
Habitat: Gardens / hedgerows / woodland margins
Food: Insects / seeds during winter
Islands status: Resident G/A/JS

Dunnocks, or hedge accentors, are a retiring little bird often described as skulking. This is a reputation earned through its habit of feeding mostly on the ground in thick cover. They are insectivores but as seeds become available through the seasons, they tend to prefer them. In winter the dunnock can often be seen on lawns gleaning seeds which fall from the bird table.

Robin

Latin name: *Erithacus rubecula*
Habitat: Gardens / hedgerows / woodland margins
Food: Insects / berries / worms
Islands status: Resident G/A/J/S

Robins are best seen in winter when the leaves are off the trees. They are regular visitors to the garden bird table and will happily keep company with gardeners in spring and autumn when disturbed ground produces the worms and insects upon which they feed. In complete contrast to this bold human contact, robins become somewhat reclusive during the breeding season. Numbers increase considerably during the autumn when local birds are joined by northern migrants.

Blackbird

Latin name: *Turdus merula*
Habitat: Gardens / hedgerows /
woodland margins
Food: Insects / berries / worms
Islands status: Resident G/A/J/S

Blackbirds are very common in the islands and
are found in a variety of habitats. Few people
fail to identify the male with confidence –
sooty black with a bright yellow bill, and one
of Britain's best songsters. The female is dark
brown with a slightly paler breast. In woods, shrubberies and dense
undergrowth they can often be heard shuffling through dead leaves in search
of worms and insects.

Song thrush

Latin name: *Turdus philomelos*
Habitat: Gardens / hedgerows / woodland margins
Food: Fruit / berries / worms / snails
Islands status: Resident G/A/J/S

The song thrush is still fairly common throughout the islands,
although in recent years there has been a noticeable reduction
in numbers. Above, the song thrush is an earthy-brown
coloured bird; the bill is brown and the chin and breast a delicate
creamy yellow, beautifully marked with lines of dark brown spots. In autumn
and winter, the berries of holly, ivy, hawthorn and elder are great favourites.

Greenfinch

Latin name: *Carduelis chloris*
Habitat: Open woodland / farmland / gardens
Food: Seeds / berries
Islands status: Resident A/G/J/S

The male greenfinch is an artist's palette of greens,
greys and yellows. The brilliant yellow flashes on the
outer tail feathers and primary wing feathers are
quite striking in both summer and winter, especially
when the bird is in flight or being belligerent at the
bird table.

Chaffinch

Latin name: *Fringilla coelebs*
Habitat: Farmland / gardens / hedgerows
Food: Seeds / berries / fruit
Islands status: Resident A/G/J Winter visitor S

It is estimated that between ten and twenty
million chaffinches arrive in Britain from the
north and east each autumn and certainly the islands receive
their fair share. The plumage of the male bird is distinctive, with the head
and neck a smoky-blue, and the mantle a rich brown merging into green
on the rump. The breast is pale reddish-pink and the wings have double
white wing-bars.

Barn swallow

Latin name: *Hirundo rustica*
Habitat: Parkland / farmland / wetland areas
Food: Flying insects
Islands status: Summer resident G/A/J/S

The first swallows are always seen as an indication of
the imminent arrival of summer. Many hundreds
complete the long journey from South Africa to make
their nests and raise their young in local barns, garages
and out-houses. Best recognised by their long tail
streamers, these small streamlined birds have metallic-blue
plumage above, a white breast and chestnut coloured facial markings.

House martin

Latin name: *Delichon urbica*
Habitat: Parkland / farmland
Food: Flying insects
Islands status: Summer resident G/A/J/S

House martins usually arrive from central
and southern Africa at the same time of year as the
swallow. The tail is much less forked than the swallow's
and the bird is probably best recognised by its blue-black
plumage and striking white rump. House martins make an
intricate rounded nest made up of mud and grasses, usually
under the eaves of houses. House martins often have two or
sometimes three broods each year.

Barn owl

Latin name: *Tyto alba*
Habitat: Parkland / farmland
Food: Small mammals
Islands status:
Resident A/G/J

Barn owls in the Channel
Islands did not suffer so serious a
decline in numbers as was
experienced on the British
mainland some years ago but
their difficulties were added to
by Dutch Elm disease which
destroyed a great many of
their traditional breeding sites.
The recent installation of a
large number of nest boxes
has helped to alleviate the
problem and although not all
are used for breeding, some
provide useful roosting sites.

Black-headed gull

Latin name: *Larus ridibundus*
Habitat: Parkland / farmland
Food: Fish / crustaceans / carrion / insects and their larvae
Islands status: Winter visitor A/G/J/S

Winter

Many thousands of black-headed gulls winter in the islands and
because their diet includes a high proportion of worms and
grubs, they are as common inland as on the coast.
In autumn they begin to lose their
chocolate-brown hoods and by winter only
a small, dark comma-shaped mark remains
behind the eye. The legs and bill are bright
red and the wing tips are black. The back is of the palest
blue-grey and the under-wings, seen best in flight, are a
smoky-grey.

Carrion crow

Latin name: *Corvus corone*
Habitat: Almost all habitats
Food: Omnivorous
Islands status: Resident A/G/J/S

The carrion crow is a very common island resident and flocks of non-breeding birds are also present throughout the year in small groups along coastal cliffs, beaches and agricultural land. The carrion crow is an all-black bird from the tip of its bill to the powerful feet and male and female are alike. Inland, seeds, berries, mammals, reptiles, acorns, worms and insects all play a part in their diet. Although the carrion crow shows a preference for nesting high in mature trees, cliff crevices and old quarries are also chosen on occasion.

Magpie

Latin name: *Pica pica*
Habitat: Almost all habitats
Food: Omnivorous
Islands status: Resident A/G/J/S

Magpies are members of the crow family and are very common Channel Island residents. They nest in trees and mature, usually dense, shrubs such as hawthorn and are one of the very few species which builds a roofed nest. The magpie is Britain's only large black and white resident bird with a tail almost as long as its body. Bold white patches below the mantle, a white belly and white primary feathers contrast strikingly with the bird's black head, upper parts, breast, bill and legs. Seen in good light, the tail is a beautiful iridescent green.

Pied wagtail

Latin name: *Motacilla alba*
Habitat: Almost all habitats
Food: Omnivorous
Islands status: Winter visitor and migrant A/G/J/S

Pied wagtails are very common winter visitors. During the day they
can be found wherever there is an abundant supply of the flies
and other insects which form their diet. They roost communally
in a variety of places offering protection from strong winds. Piles
of seaweed on the high tide line are perhaps the best place to find them.

Common Pheasant

Latin name: *Phasianus colchicus*
Habitat: Farmland / rough grassland / woodland margins
Food: Grain / seeds / fruit / insects / worms / slugs
Islands status: Resident A/G/J/S

The common pheasant has been introduced to the Channel Islands
on numerous occasions and is currently present in all the islands
although scarce in Alderney and Sark.
Due largely to birds being release in considerable numbers,
the Jersey population has grown to the extent that they
are now regarded as a common species and are
present in all parishes.
These delightful and rather exotic looking
birds were originally introduced into
England by the Normans during the
11th Century. Despite their size, they
have the ability to use cover to
advantage and are often heard
rather than seen.

Index

Notes